Team Spirit

THE SEATTLE MARINERS

BY

MARK STEWART

Content Consultant
James L. Gates, Jr.
Library Director
National Baseball Hall of Fame and Museum

NORWOOD HOUSE PRESS

CHICAGO, ILLINOIS

Norwood House Press
P.O. Box 316598
Chicago, Illinois 60631

For information regarding Norwood House Press, please visit our website at:
www.norwoodhousepress.com or call 866-565-2900.

PHOTO CREDITS:
All photos courtesy of AP Images—AP/Wide World Photos, Inc., except the following:
Author's Collection (7, 20, 21 both, 29, 34 bottom right, 35 top left, 43);
John Klein (8, 9, 17, 22, 23 top, top right and bottom left);
Topps, Inc. (14, 34 top and bottom left, 40 top and bottom left);
Photofest (36); Classic Games, Inc. (39).

Editor: Mike Kennedy
Designer: Ron Jaffe
Project Management: Black Book Partners, LLC.

Special thanks to Rob McDermott Hale.

Library of Congress Cataloging-in-Publication Data

Stewart, Mark, 1960-
   The Seattle Mariners / by Mark Stewart ; content consultant James L.
Gates, Jr.
      p. cm. -- (Team spirit)
   Summary: "Presents the history, accomplishments and key personalities of
the Seattle Mariners baseball team. Includes timelines, quotes, maps,
glossary and websites"--Provided by publisher.
   Includes bibliographical references and index.
   ISBN-13: 978-1-59953-097-0 (library edition : alk. paper)
   ISBN-10: 1-59953-097-X (library edition : alk. paper)
   1. Seattle Mariners (Baseball team)--Juvenile literature. I. Gates, Jr., James L.
II. Title.
GV875.S42S74 2007
796.357'6409797772--dc22
                                                    2006033024

COVER PHOTO: The Mariners congratulate each other
after a victory during the 2005 season.

Table of Contents

SPORTS WORDS & VOCABULARY WORDS: In this book, you will find many words that are new to you. You may also see familiar words used in new ways. The glossary on page 46 gives the meanings of baseball words, as well as "everyday" words that have special baseball meanings. These words appear in **bold type** throughout the book. The glossary on page 47 gives the meanings of vocabulary words that are not related to baseball. They appear in ***bold italic type*** throughout the book.

Meet the Mariners

When you say the word "sports" in most cities, people think of the town's favorite teams and best players. In Seattle, Washington it means much more. Outdoor sports such as hiking, boating, and mountain biking are an important part of people's lives. This is how they feel close to nature. When sports fans in the **Pacific Northwest** want to feel close to each *other*, they buy a ticket to watch the Mariners play.

The Mariners have had their ups and downs over the years, but their fans have always been loyal. The team has rewarded them by putting some of the game's most unusual and talented players on the field.

This book tells the story of the Mariners. While they may be just one part of Seattle's sports picture, they occupy an important place in the city's heart. In a region where people love to meet challenges, the Mariners have met their own challenges with amazing victories and record-breaking seasons.

Ichiro Suzuki watches Raul Ibanez "high-five" Yuniesky Betancourt as the Mariners leave the field after a victory.

Way Back When

The people of Seattle have loved baseball for more than a century. For many seasons, they rooted for a **minor-league** team called the Rainiers. In 1969, Seattle's fans were thrilled when their city joined the **American League (A.L.)** with a new team called the Pilots. The excitement turned to sadness a year later, when the team moved to Milwaukee, Wisconsin and became the Brewers. The A.L. promised that Seattle would get a new team, and the city promised that the new team would have a magnificent new stadium.

In 1977, the A.L. added two more teams, the Mariners and the Toronto Blue Jays. The Mariners built their team by choosing unwanted players from other clubs, and by **drafting** players from high school and college. The Mariners moved into a new stadium called the Kingdome. They shared it with the Seattle Supersonics basketball team and Seattle Seahawks football team.

The Mariners continued to search for players who had been overlooked by other teams. In their early years, their hitting stars included Ruppert Jones, Dan Meyer, Leroy Stanton, Bruce Bochte, Leon Roberts, Willie Horton, Ken Phelps, and Al Cowens. Their best pitchers were Glenn Abbott, Rick Honeycutt, and Bill Caudill. Later the Mariners began relying on their minor-league teams to supply talent.

In the mid-1980s, the Mariners had a group of "homegrown" stars who were ready to take over. The best was Mark Langston, a left-handed pitcher who led the league in strikeouts as a **rookie**. First baseman Alvin Davis, second baseman Harold Reynolds, third baseman Jim Presley, and outfielder Phil Bradley gave the team a solid **lineup**.

Even with this talent, the Mariners did not have their first winning season until 1991. By then, they were building a new team around an amazing young outfielder named Ken Griffey Jr. He would lead the A.L. in home runs four times and win 10 **Gold Glove** awards.

LEFT: The Kingdome, the first home of the Mariners.
ABOVE: Al Cowens, one of Seattle's early stars.

Randy Johnson also joined the Mariners during this time. He was a tall, left-handed pitcher who whipped the ball in at terrifying speeds. Johnson pitched Seattle's first **no-hitter** in 1990, and led the A.L. in strikeouts four years in a row. Other Seattle stars during the 1990s included Edgar Martinez, Jay Buhner, Tino Martinez, and Alex Rodriguez.

The Mariners were managed by Lou Piniella during this period. He led the team to the **American League Championship Series (ALCS)** twice, but both times Seattle fell short of winning the **pennant**. In 1998, this team of stars began to break up. Some players had grown old, while others were injured. Johnson was traded, then Griffey was traded, too. When Rodriguez left Seattle after the 2000 season, even the most loyal fans wondered when the Mariners would have a good team again.

LEFT: Ken Griffey Jr. loved playing for the Mariners. He was the team's best player in the 1990s.
ABOVE: Alex Rodriguez, one of Seattle's greatest players ever.

The Team Today

Some baseball teams win by depending on two or three superstars. Other teams play better when everyone shares the responsibility for winning. In 2001, the Mariners discovered that they could be successful both ways. After losing the three greatest players in their history—Randy Johnson, Ken Griffey Jr., and Alex Rodriguez—Seattle fans watched in amazement as their team won 116 games. This set a new A.L. record.

The Mariners were led by Ichiro Suzuki, a player from Japan in his first year in the **major leagues**. He led the A.L. in hits, stolen bases, and batting average. Bret Boone, a 32-year-old second baseman, led the league with 141 **runs batted in (RBIs)**. Jamie Moyer, a 38-year-old pitcher, won 20 games for the first time in his life.

Today's Mariners learned an important lesson from that team. If everyone contributes, the result can be record-smashing—whether you have young superstars in the lineup or not.

The Mariners wait near home plate for the winning run to score in a 2006 game. The team likes to have a good mix of talent, youth, and enthusiasm.

Home Turf

The Mariners' first home was the Kingdome. The dome protected fans and players from rainy weather, which occurs often in the Pacific Northwest. For many years, the Kingdome's 23-foot right field wall was the second-highest in baseball, after the "Green Monster" in Boston's Fenway Park. In 1999, the Mariners moved to a new stadium, Safeco Field.

Safeco Field has a ***retractable*** roof made of three panels, which slide into place when rain is in the ***forecast***. Unlike other fields with this kind of cover, Safeco is not totally enclosed when the roof is shut. Air flows through the sides of the building, so fans inside feel like they are still "outside."

SAFECO FIELD BY THE NUMBERS

- *There are 46,621 seats in the Mariners' ballpark.*
- *The distance from home plate to the left field foul pole is 331 feet.*
- *The distance from home plate to the center field fence is 405 feet.*
- *The distance from home plate to the right field foul pole is 326 feet.*
- *The stadium's roof is designed to absorb lightning strikes, hold more than six feet of snow, and withstand winds of up to 70 miles per hour.*

When the roof is open at Safeco Field, the Mariners can celebrate big moments with fireworks displays.

Dressed for Success

Seattle is one of the largest *ports* in North America. When the Mariners first announced their name, fans were happy that it linked the team to the sea. For their first 10 seasons, the M in Mariners was formed by the three points of a trident, the spear belonging to Neptune, an ancient god of the sea. The team colors were blue and yellow.

In 1987, the Mariners stopped using the trident M design and switched to a yellow S on their caps. In 1993, the team started using a design featuring the points of a *compass*. This *logo* represents the sea, technology, and the great outdoors. Each is an important part of life in the Pacific Northwest. The Mariners also switched their team colors that year to navy blue, silver, and dark green.

Dan Meyer models the team's trident logo from the 1970s.

The baseball uniform has not changed much since the Mariners began playing. It has four main parts:

- a cap or batting helmet with a sun visor
- a top with a player's number on the back
- pants that reach down between the ankle and the knee
- stirrup-style socks

The uniform top sometimes has a player's name on the back. The team's name, city, or logo is usually on the front. Baseball teams wear light-colored uniforms when they play at home, and darker styles when they play on the road.

For more than 100 years, baseball uniforms were made of wool *flannel* and were very baggy. This helped the sweat *evaporate* and gave players the freedom to move around. Today's uniforms are made of *synthetic* fabrics that stretch with players and keep them dry and cool.

Adrian Beltre runs the bases in Seattle's 2006 home uniform.

We Won!

he Mariners played their first 14 years without having a winning season. In 1991, the team finally won more games than it lost, but still finished fifth in the **A.L. West**. It took four more years before Seattle could claim its first division crown—but as any Mariners fan will tell you, it was worth the wait.

For most of that exciting 1995 season, it looked as if the California Angels would win the A.L. West. They built a big lead over the Mariners, who had lost Ken Griffey Jr. for 90 games with a broken wrist. The hitting of Edgar Martinez and pitching of Randy Johnson kept Seattle close, and when "Junior" returned, the Mariners were able to catch the Angels.

The two teams played one final game to decide who would go to the **playoffs** and who would go home. Johnson, who led the A.L. in strikeouts and **earned run average (ERA)**, was picked by manager

Lou Piniella to start this important game. Johnson pitched a masterpiece, and the Mariners were A.L. West champions.

The Mariners then met the New York Yankees in the **Division Series**. The first team to win three games would play for the pennant in the ALCS. The Yankees won the first two games, and suddenly Seattle had its back against the wall.

Johnson beat the Yankees in Game Three. The Mariners kept fighting back to win Game Four, 11–8. Martinez was the hitting hero, with seven RBIs. Game Five was one of the most tense, hardest-played games in baseball history. The fans in the Kingdome were on the edge of their seats all night.

The Yankees built a 4–2 lead, but the Mariners tied the score in the eighth inning. The Yankees loaded the bases in the ninth inning with no outs. Piniella called Johnson into the game. The exhausted pitcher faced three of baseball's toughest hitters—Wade Boggs, Bernie Williams, and Paul O'Neill—and got a strikeout and two pop-ups to save the day.

The Yankees scored a run in the 11th inning to take a 5–4 lead, and once again the Mariners found themselves facing the end of their

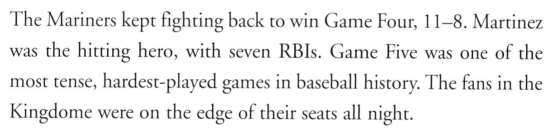

LEFT: Randy Johnson throws a fastball during the 1995 playoffs. His great pitching helped the Mariners defeat the New York Yankees.
ABOVE: Edgar Martinez, the hitting star of the 1995 playoffs.

season. At this point, they simply refused to lose. Joey Cora reached first base safely on a **bunt**, and then Griffey lined a single to center field. The next batter, Martinez, smashed the ball over third base and into left field. Cora scored easily. Griffey, running faster than he ever had in his life, rounded second base and looked into the eyes of the third base coach, Sam Perlozzo. Both men knew that there was no way Griffey was stopping—he was going to score. He slid into home plate ahead of the throw, and the Mariners came rushing out of the dugout to celebrate the winning run. It was, and still is, the greatest moment in team history.

ABOVE: Ken Griffey Jr. slides home with the winning run against the Yankees in Game Five.   **RIGHT**: Griffey finds himself at the bottom of a pile of happy Mariners.

Go-To Guys

To be a true star in baseball, you need more than a quick bat and a strong arm. You have to be a "go-to guy"—someone the manager wants on the pitcher's mound or in the batter's box when it matters most. Mariners fans have had a lot to cheer about over the years, including these great stars...

THE PIONEERS

JULIO CRUZ — Second Baseman

• BORN: 12/2/1954 • PLAYED FOR TEAM: 1977 TO 1983

Julio Cruz was the man who made the Mariners go in their early years. He stole 290 bases for Seattle—including 32 in a row from 1980 to 1981.

MARK LANGSTON — Pitcher

• BORN: 8/20/1960 • PLAYED FOR TEAM: 1984 TO 1989

Mark Langston overpowered hitters with a blazing fastball. He led the A.L. in strikeouts three times, including his first season. Only three other rookies had done this before.

ALVIN DAVIS — First Baseman

• BORN: 9/9/1960 • PLAYED FOR TEAM: 1984 TO 1991

In 1984, Alvin Davis became the first Mariner to win a major award when he was named **Rookie of the Year**. He had a powerful swing and a sharp batting eye.

HAROLD REYNOLDS — Second Baseman

- BORN: 11/26/1960
- PLAYED FOR TEAM: 1983 TO 1992

When Harold Reynolds stole 60 bases in 1987, he became the first Mariner to lead the A.L. in an important **offensive** category. He was also one of the best fielders in the game.

EDGAR MARTINEZ — Designated Hitter/Third Baseman

- BORN: 1/2/1963
- PLAYED FOR TEAM: 1987 TO 2004

Edgar Martinez led the A.L. in batting average twice and **on-base percentage** three times. In 1995, he became the first designated hitter (DH) to win a batting championship.

JAY BUHNER — Outfielder

- BORN: 8/13/1964
- PLAYED FOR TEAM: 1988 TO 2001

For many years, Jay Buhner was the "glue" that held the Mariners together. He was a great team player, and the first Mariner to hit 40 home runs three years in a row.

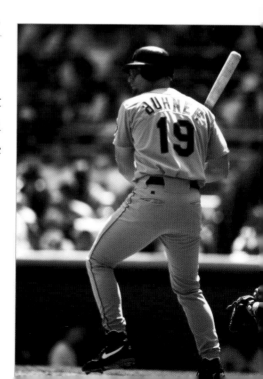

LEFT: Mark Langston
TOP RIGHT: Edgar Martinez
BOTTOM RIGHT: Jay Buhner

MODERN STARS

KEN GRIFFEY JR.   Outfielder

- BORN: 11/21/1969 • PLAYED FOR TEAM: 1989 TO 1999

Ken Griffey Jr. was the best **all-around** player in baseball when he wore a Seattle uniform. "Junior" led the A.L. in home runs four times between 1994 and 1999, and hit 56 home runs twice in a row. He was also the best defensive outfielder in the league.

RANDY JOHNSON   Pitcher

- BORN: 9/10/1963

- PLAYED FOR TEAM: 1989 TO 1998

At 6' 10", Randy Johnson was the tallest player in baseball when he pitched for the Mariners. The "Big Unit" threw the team's first no-hitter in 1990 and won the **Cy Young Award** in 1995.

BRET BOONE   Second Baseman

- BORN: 4/6/1969

- PLAYED FOR TEAM: 1992 TO 1993 & 2001 TO 2005

The Mariners traded Bret Boone away when he was just 24, and then finally got him back seven years later. He rewarded them by having one of the greatest seasons ever by an A.L. second baseman, with 206 hits, 37 home runs, and 141 RBIs.

ALEX RODRIGUEZ — Shortstop

- BORN: 7/27/1975 • PLAYED FOR TEAM: 1994 TO 2000

When Alex Rodriguez hit .358 in 1996, it was the highest batting average ever by a player who started a season younger than 21. "A-Rod" became an excellent power hitter, fielder, and baserunner during his years with the Mariners.

ICHIRO SUZUKI — Outfielder

- BORN: 10/22/1973 • FIRST YEAR WITH TEAM: 2001

Only a handful of players have won the Rookie of the Year and **Most Valuable Player (MVP)** awards in their career. Ichiro Suzuki won them *both* in his first season with the Mariners. In 2004, he used his slashing swing and great speed to set a new record with 262 hits in a season.

FELIX HERNANDEZ — Pitcher

- BORN: 4/8/1986 • FIRST YEAR WITH TEAM: 2005

Felix Hernandez was just 19 when he first pitched for the Mariners, but he already looked like an experienced star. He could throw his fastball and curveball to every part of the strike zone, and was very cool under pressure.

LEFT: Randy Johnson
TOP RIGHT: Alex Rodriguez
BOTTOM RIGHT: Felix Hernandez

On the Sidelines

The Mariners have had many managers since they started in 1977. Because the team has always mixed older, experienced players with young players who are still learning the game, the job of managing Seattle has often been a complicated one. How do you get the same point across to the players who know very little, as well as players who think they "know it all"?

The best managers for the Mariners have been the ones who communicate clearly with their players, and who have a history of winning. No matter what a player's age or experience, these are the things rookies and veterans respect most in a leader.

Seattle's most successful manager was Lou Piniella. The Mariners knew he had won championships as a player and manager, and they saw that he poured his heart into every game. They had seven winning seasons with Piniella in the dugout, and reached the ALCS in 1995 and 2000.

Manager Mike Hargrove congratulates 19-year-old Felix Hernandez after his first game in 2005. The Mariners try to hire experienced leaders such as Hargrove to guide young players like Hernandez.

One Great Day

itting a home run takes skill, strength, great *coordination*, and perfect timing. It also takes a little luck. Think about how hard it would be for one player to hit four home runs in the same game. Before Mike Cameron of the Mariners took the field against the Chicago White Sox on a spring evening in 2002, only three American

Leaguers had ever done this. He would soon become the fourth.

In the first inning, Cameron swung at a fastball from starting pitcher Jon Rauch and hit it out of the park. Later in that same inning, Cameron came up again against **relief pitcher** Jim Parque—and hit another ball over the fence! Seattle's second baseman, Bret Boone, also hit two home runs in the first inning. This was the first time in history two teammates had each hit two home runs in the same inning.

Cameron was not finished. He came up again in the third inning against Parque and hit another ball into the stands for his third home run of the game. Two innings later, poor Parque was still on the mound when Cameron stepped into the batter's box for the fourth time. Sure enough, the Mariners' **slugger** hit home run number four.

No one had ever hit five home runs in a major-league game. Cameron hoped to be the first. In the seventh inning, he was hit by a pitch from Mike Porzio. In the ninth inning, he drove a pitch by Porzio to the right field fence, but Jeff Liefer caught it.

"I tried to go for it," Cameron smiled after the game. In the Chicago locker room, Rauch and Parque were not smiling. They were told to pack their bags—they had been sent back to the minor leagues.

LEFT: Mike Cameron trots around third base after his first home run against the White Sox.   **RIGHT** : Cameron hits his third home run of the game.

Legend Has It

Who was the best "baseball grandson" in major-league history?

LEGEND HAS IT that it was Bret Boone. Boone's father, Bob, was one of the game's top catchers for many years. He played in four **All-Star Games** during his career. Bob's father, Ray, was an All-Star third baseman. He led the A.L. in RBIs in 1955. Forty-six years later, Ray cheered on his grandson, Bret, as he led the A.L. in RBIs as a member of the 2001 Mariners.

How did Ichiro learn such great bat control?

LEGEND HAS IT that his dad taught him. When Ichiro was a boy, his father, Nobuyuki Suzuki, would kneel just a few feet in front of home plate. As he tossed baseballs to his son—high, low, inside, and outside—Ichiro had to decide quickly where to hit the ball without hitting his father. In all the years they played this game, Ichiro never hit him once!

Did anyone ever see "Bigfoot" at a Mariners game?

LEGEND HAS IT that they did—52 times! In 1986, Pete "Bigfoot" Ladd pitched in 52 games for the Mariners. It was not hard to understand how he got this nickname. Ladd stood 6' 3" and weighed 240 pounds. He had long, tangled hair, a bushy mustache, and enormous feet. He could be one scary dude! During the winters, when many players took long vacations, Ladd kept himself busy as a prison guard in his home state of Maine.

Pete Ladd thought the nickname "Bigfoot" was a good fit.

It Really Happened

There was no prouder father in baseball than Ken Griffey Sr. when the 1990 season began. The 40-year-old outfielder for the Cincinnati Reds was the only man in the major leagues who could say his son was a major leaguer too. In fact, it was the first time in history that any **active player** could say this.

Ken Griffey Jr. was in his second season with the Mariners and having a great year as the team's center fielder. On August 29th, "Junior" learned that a new left fielder was joining the team—his father!

Two days later, they were in the lineup together against the Kansas City Royals. Ken Sr. hit a single **up the middle** in the first inning, and then challenged his son to match him. Ken Jr. did as his father told him, and hit a single to right field. In a game on September 14th against the California Angels, the Griffeys were at it again. They hit back-to-back home runs!

When the season ended, Ken Jr. had a .300 average. How did Ken Sr. do? He batted .377 in 21 games for the Mariners. The Griffeys played one more season together, in 1991. In all, father and son were on the same lineup card more than 50 times.

LEFT: The Griffeys have a father-and-son catch before a game in Chicago.
RIGHT: Once his playing days ended, Ken Griffey Sr. watched his son play as often as he could.

Team Spirit

Seattle fans love their sports teams and have a special connection with their players. Their greatest wish is for the athletes who live and play in the city to feel like part of the community. They want them to believe, as they do, that the lifestyle of the Pacific Northwest has just the right mix of excitement and *tranquility*.

At Mariners games, the fans are hardly ever tranquil. They cheer loudly for every hit and out, and let the players know Seattle appreciates them. The crowd also enjoys some of baseball's best food and music.

The Seattle area has many Japanese-American residents and visitors from Japan who are baseball fans. The Mariners often look for Japanese stars who want to play in the United States. Over the years, players such as Kazuhiro Sasaki, Ichiro Suzuki, and Kenji Johjima have been able to prove themselves in the major leagues—and win games for the Mariners.

The fans at Safeco Field cheer for Yuniesky Betancourt, whose journey to Seattle was long and dangerous. He fled Cuba on a raft in 2003 for the chance to play baseball in the United States.

Timeline

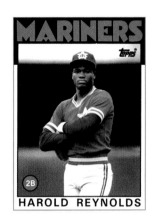

Harold
Reynolds

1977
The Mariners play
their first game
on April 6th.

1982
Gaylord Perry wins his
300th game as a member
of the Mariners.

1987
Harold Reynolds leads
the A.L. with 60
stolen bases.

1979
The All-Star Game is played
in Seattle's Kingdome.

1984
Alvin Davis is named
A.L. Rookie of the Year.

1991
The Mariners
have their first
winning season.

Bruce Bochte, who
got a hit for the
home fans during the
1979 All-Star Game.

Alvin
Davis

Jay Buhner led the 1995 Mariners with 40 home runs and 121 RBIs.

Ken Griffey Jr.

1995
The Mariners win the A.L. West for the first time.

1998
Ken Griffey Jr. leads the A.L. with 56 home runs.

2001
The Mariners set an A.L. record with 116 victories.

1994
Randy Johnson leads the A.L. in strikeouts.

1996
Alex Rodriguez is the first A.L. shortstop to win a batting championship in 52 years.

2006
Ichiro Suzuki becomes the first player to start his career with six 200-hit seasons.

Alex Rodriguez

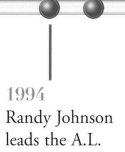

Ichiro Suzuki

Fun Facts

SPECIAL KAYE

The Mariners' first owners were Lester Smith and Danny Kaye. Kaye was a famous actor who loved baseball.

NUMBER ONE DAD

When Ken Griffey Sr. joined the Mariners in 1990, he asked Matt Young if he would be willing to give up number 30. Young agreed, and became one of the only pitchers in history to wear number 1. His eight-year-old daughter, Brynn, chose the number.

BIG BANG

The team's first home, the Kingdome, was demolished in 2000 to make room for a new football stadium. It took 5,800 dynamite charges to bring down the building, which fell in just 20 seconds.

BUSY BULLPEN

In a 1992 game against the Texas Rangers, the Mariners set a record by using 11 different pitchers.

FIRST NAME FIRST

Ichiro Suzuki was the first player in both Japanese and American baseball to have his first name (instead of his last) on the back of his uniform.

BETTER LUCK NEXT TIME

Ten-year-old Ken Griffey Jr. played his first Little League season without making an out. When he made his first out at age 11, he cried.

BAD START, NICE FINISH

In a 1993 game against the Boston Red Sox, Chris Bosio walked the first two batters he faced. He then got 27 outs in a row for a no-hitter.

LEFT: Danny Kaye talks baseball on the Mariners' bench in 1977.
TOP RIGHT: Everyone knows Ichiro by his first name.
BOTTOM RIGHT: Chris Bosio with Lou Piniella, who hired Bosio as a coach after his playing days.

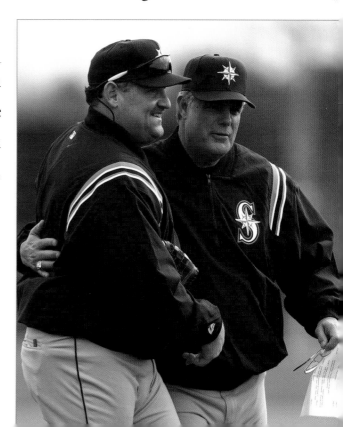

Talking Baseball

"You know who I play for? I play for the kids ... I just like to see them laughing and happy—just as *I* always want to be."

—*Ken Griffey Jr., on his favorite fans*

"I wanted the challenge of competing against the best players in the world."

—*Ichiro Suzuki, on why he joined the Mariners after winning seven batting championships in Japan*

"When you can throw 97 miles an hour and put the ball over the plate anytime you want, it's fun."

—Randy Johnson, on the joy of pitching with speed and control

"You always dream about being on a baseball card. It's kind of funny when you finally see it."

—Alex Rodriguez, on seeing himself on his first trading card

"The more in tune the pitcher and catcher are, the better the chance they're going to succeed. I think it's trust."

—Lou Piniella, on the key to a well-pitched game

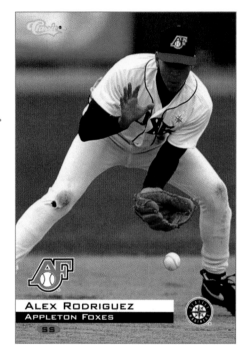

ALEX RODRIGUEZ
APPLETON FOXES
SS

"Seattle is where I wanted to be ... it's where I've always wanted to be. It feels like home to me."

—Raul Ibanez, on returning to the Mariners after three years playing for another team

LEFT: Ken Griffey Jr. signs a copy of his book *Junior: Griffey on Griffey* for a young fan.   **ABOVE**: Alex Rodriguez's first trading card shows him as a minor leaguer.

For the Record

T he great Mariners teams and players have left their marks on the record books. These are the "best of the best"…

MARINERS AWARD WINNERS

WINNER	AWARD	YEAR
Alvin Davis	Rookie of the Year	1984
Ken Griffey Jr.	All-Star Game MVP	1992
Randy Johnson	Cy Young Award	1995
Lou Piniella	Manager of the Year	1995
Ken Griffey Jr.	Most Valuable Player	1997
Kazuhiro Sasaki	Rookie of the Year	2000
Lou Piniella	Manager of the Year	2001
Ichiro Suzuki	Rookie of the Year	2001
Ichiro Suzuki	Most Valuable Player	2001

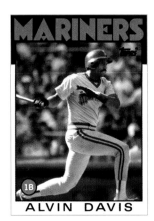

Randy Johnson

Alvin Davis

Ichiro Suzuki is congratulated by fellow Japanese star Kenji Johjima.

MARINERS ACHIEVEMENTS

ACHIEVEMENT	YEAR
A.L. West Champions	1995
A.L. West Champions	1997
A.L. Wild Card	2000
A.L. West Champions	2001

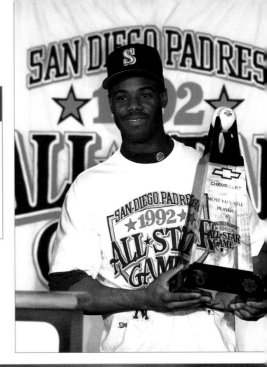

RIGHT: Ken Griffey Jr. with his 1992 All-Star Game MVP trophy.   **BELOW**: Jay Buhner honors Kazuhiro Sasaki with a traditional bow. The Japanese pitcher was named Rookie of the Year in 2000.

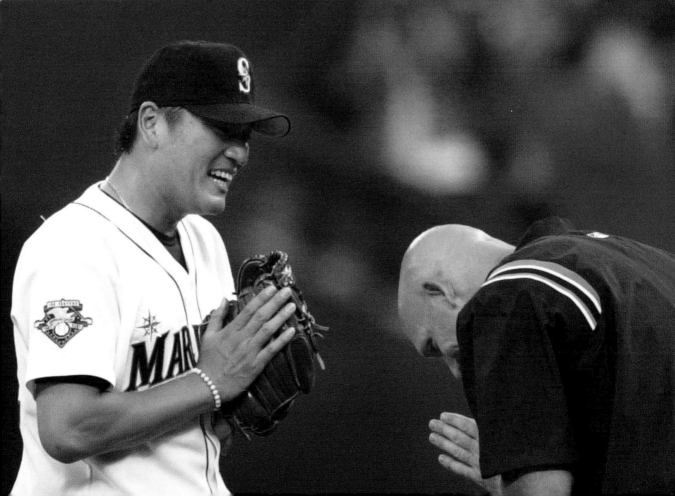

Pinpoints

The history of a baseball team is made up of many smaller stories. These stories take place all over the map—not just in the city a team calls "home." Match the push-pins on these maps to the Team Facts and you will begin to see the story of the Mariners unfold!

TEAM FACTS

1. Seattle, Washington—*The team has played here since 1977.*
2. El Cajon, California—*Bret Boone was born here.*
3. Little Rock, Arkansas—*Glenn Abbott was born here.*
4. Bloomington, Indiana—*Phil Bradley was born here.*
5. Hamilton, Ohio—*Dan Meyer was born here.*
6. Donora, Pennsylvania—*Ken Griffey Jr. was born here.*
7. New York, New York—*Alex Rodriguez was born here.*
8. Arno, Virginia—*Willie Horton was born here.*
9. Williamston, North Carolina—*Gaylord Perry was born here.*
10. Tampa, Florida—*Lou Piniella was born here.*
11. Valencia, Venezuela—*Felix Hernandez was born here.*
12. Kasugai, Japan—*Ichiro Suzuki was born here.*

Phil Bradley

43

Play Ball

Baseball is a game played between two teams over nine innings. Teams take one turn at bat and one turn in the field during each inning. A turn at bat ends when three outs are made. The batters on the hitting team try to reach base safely. The players on the fielding team try to prevent this from happening.

In baseball, the ball is controlled by the pitcher. The pitcher must throw the ball to the batter, who decides whether or not to swing at each pitch. If a batter swings and misses, it is a strike. If the batter lets a good pitch go by, it is also a strike. If the batter swings and the ball does not stay in fair territory (between the v-shaped lines that begin at home plate) it is called "foul," and is counted as a strike. If the pitcher throws three strikes, the batter is out. If the pitcher throws four bad pitches before that, the batter is awarded first base. This is called a base-on-balls, or "walk."

When the batter swings the bat and hits the ball, everyone springs into action. If a fielder catches a batted ball before it hits the ground, the batter is out. If a fielder scoops the ball off the ground and throws it to first base before the batter arrives, the batter is out. If the batter reaches first base safely, he is credited with a hit. A one-base hit is called a single, a two-base hit is called a double, a three-base hit is called a triple, and a four-base hit is called a home run.

Runners who reach base are only safe when they are touching one of the bases. If they are caught between the bases, the fielders can tag them with the ball and record an out.

A batter who is able to circle the bases and make it back to home plate before three outs are made is credited with a run scored. The team with the most runs after nine innings is the winner.

Anyone who has played baseball (or softball) knows that it can be a complicated game. Every player on the field has a job to do. Different players have different strengths and weaknesses. The pitchers, batters, and managers make hundreds of decisions every game. The more you play and watch baseball, the more "little things" you are likely to notice. The next time you are at a game, look for these plays:

PLAY LIST

DOUBLE PLAY—A play where the fielding team is able to make two outs on one batted ball. This usually happens when a runner is on first base, and the batter hits a ground ball to one of the infielders. The base runner is forced out at second base and the ball is then thrown to first base before the batter arrives.

HIT AND RUN—A play where the runner on first base sprints to second base while the pitcher is throwing the ball to the batter. When the second baseman or shortstop moves toward the base to wait for the catcher's throw, the batter tries to hit the ball to the place that the fielder has just left. If the batter swings and misses, the fielding team can tag the runner out.

INTENTIONAL WALK—A play when the pitcher throws four bad pitches on purpose, allowing the batter to walk to first base. This happens when the pitcher would much rather face the next batter—and is willing to risk putting a runner on base.

SACRIFICE BUNT—A play where the batter makes an out on purpose so that a teammate can move to the next base. On a bunt, the batter tries to "deaden" the pitch with the bat instead of swinging at it.

SHOESTRING CATCH—A play where an outfielder catches a short hit an inch or two above the ground, near the tops of his shoes. It is not easy to run as fast as you can and lower your glove without slowing down. It can be risky, too. If a fielder misses a shoestring catch, the ball might roll all the way to the fence.

Glossary

BASEBALL WORDS TO KNOW

ACTIVE PLAYER—Someone who is on a major-league team.

ALL-AROUND—Good at all parts of the game.

ALL-STAR GAMES—The annual midsummer meetings between the best players in the American and National Leagues. The winner is awarded home-field advantage in that fall's World Series.

A.L. WEST—A division in the American League made up of teams located in the western part of the country.

AMERICAN LEAGUE (A.L.)—One of baseball's two major leagues. The A.L. started play in 1901. The National League began play in 1876.

AMERICAN LEAGUE CHAMPIONSHIP SERIES (ALCS)—The competition that has decided the American League pennant since 1969.

BUNT—A short hit made by "blocking" a pitch with the bat. A bunt is sometimes used by fast batters to surprise the defense.

CY YOUNG AWARD—The trophy given to each league's best pitcher each year.

DIVISION SERIES—The official name of the first round of the playoffs. The Division Series was first played in 1995.

DRAFTING—Choosing a high-school or college player.

EARNED RUN AVERAGE (ERA)—A statistic that measures how many runs a pitcher gives up for every nine innings he pitches.

GOLD GLOVE—An award given each year to baseball's best fielders.

LINEUP—The list of players who are playing in a game.

MAJOR LEAGUES—The top level of professional baseball leagues. The American League and National League make up today's major leagues. Sometimes called the "big leagues."

MINOR-LEAGUE—Belonging to one of the professional leagues that are below the major-league level.

MOST VALUABLE PLAYER (MVP)—An award given each year to each league's top player; an MVP is also selected for the World Series and All-Star Game.

NO-HITTER—A game in which one team is unable to get a hit.

OFFENSIVE—Related to hitting or scoring.

ON-BASE PERCENTAGE—A statistic that measures how often a batter reaches base on a hit or walk, or when he is hit by a pitch.

PENNANT—A league championship. The term comes from the triangular flag awarded to each season's champion, beginning in the 1870s.

PLAYOFFS—The games played after the regular season to determine which teams will advance to the World Series.

RELIEF PITCHER—A pitcher who is brought into a game to replace another pitcher. Relief pitchers can be seen warming up in the bullpen.

ROOKIE—A player in his first season.

ROOKIE OF THE YEAR—An annual award given to each league's best first-year player.

RUNS BATTED IN (RBIs)—A statistic that measures the number of runners a batter drives home.

SLUGGER—A powerful hitter.

UP THE MIDDLE—Over the pitcher's mound and second base.

OTHER WORDS TO KNOW

COMPASS—An instrument used to navigate or show direction.

COORDINATION—The working together of different muscles to perform a complex action.

EVAPORATE—Disappear, or turn into vapor.

FLANNEL—A soft wool or cotton material.

FORECAST—A prediction of future weather.

LOGO—A symbol or design that represents a company or team.

PACIFIC NORTHWEST—A region of North America that includes the states of Oregon and Washington.

PORTS—Places where ships load and unload.

RETRACTABLE—Able to pull back.

SYNTHETIC—Made in a laboratory, not in nature.

TRANQUILITY—Freedom from noise and commotion.

Places to Go

ON THE ROAD

SEATTLE MARINERS
Safeco Field
1250 First Avenue South
Seattle, Washington 98134
(206) 346-4000

NATIONAL BASEBALL HALL OF FAME AND MUSEUM
25 Main Street
Cooperstown, New York 13326
(888) 425-5633
www.baseballhalloffame.org

ON THE WEB

THE SEATTLE MARINERS   www.seattlemariners.com
 • *to learn more about the Mariners*

MAJOR LEAGUE BASEBALL   www.mlb.com
 • *to learn about all the major league teams*

MINOR LEAGUE BASEBALL   www.minorleaguebaseball.com
 • *to learn more about the minor leagues*

ON THE BOOKSHELVES

To learn more about the sport of baseball, look for these books at your library or bookstore:

 • Kelly, James. *Baseball*. New York, NY: DK, 2005.

 • Jacobs, Greg. *The Everything Kids' Baseball Book*. Cincinnati, OH: Adams Media Corporation, 2006.

 • Stewart, Mark and Kennedy, Mike. *Long Ball: The Legend and Lore of the Home Run*. Minneapolis, MN: Millbrook Press, 2006.

47

Index

The Team

MARK STEWART has written more than 25 books on baseball, and over 100 sports books for kids. He grew up in New York City during the 1960s rooting for the Yankees and Mets, and now takes his two daughters, Mariah and Rachel, to the same ballparks. Mark comes from a family of writers. His grandfather was Sunday Editor of the *New York Times* and his mother was Articles Editor of *Ladies' Home Journal* and *McCall's*. Mark has profiled hundreds of athletes over the last 20 years. He has also written several books about his native New York and New Jersey, his home today. Mark is a graduate of Duke University, with a degree in history. He lives with his daughters and wife, Sarah, overlooking Sandy Hook, NJ.

JAMES L. GATES, JR. has served as Library Director at the National Baseball Hall of Fame since 1995. He had previously served in academic libraries for almost fifteen years. He holds degrees from Belmont Abbey College, the University of Notre Dame, and Indiana University. During his career Jim has authored several academic articles and has served in an editorial capacity on multiple book, magazine, and museum publications, and he also serves as host for the Annual Cooperstown Symposium on Baseball and American Culture. He is an ardent Baltimore Orioles fan and enjoys watching baseball with his wife and two children.